EVERYTHING PRESERVED

WINNER OF THE
EMILY DICKINSON FIRST BOOK AWARD
FROM THE POETRY FOUNDATION

||||||||||||||||||||||||||||||||||||||||||||||||||||||||||||||||||||||||||||||||||||||||||

Everything Preserved:

Poems 1955 – 2005

||||||||||||||||||||||||||||||||||||||||||||||||||||||||||||||||||||||||||||||||||||||||||

LANDIS EVERSON

Edited by Ben Mazer

Graywolf Press

SAINT PAUL, MINNESOTA

Publication of this volume is made possible in part by a grant provided by the Minnesota State Arts Board, through an appropriation by the Minnesota State Legislature; a grant from the Wells Fargo Foundation Minnesota; and a grant from the National Endowment for the Arts, which believes that a great nation deserves great art. Significant support has also been provided by the Bush Foundation; Target; the McKnight Foundation; and other generous contributions from foundations, corporations, and individuals. To these organizations and individuals we offer our heartfelt thanks.

 Winner of the 2005 Emily Dickinson First Book Award established by the Poetry Foundation to recognize an American Poet over the age of 50 who has yet to publish a first book.

Published by Graywolf Press
2402 University Avenue, Suite 203
Saint Paul, Minnesota 55114
All rights reserved.

www.graywolfpress.org

Published in the United States of America
ISBN-13: 978-1-55597-453-4
ISBN-10: 1-55597-453-8

2 4 6 8 9 7 5 3 1
First Graywolf Printing, 2006

Library of Congress Control Number: 2006924341

Cover design: VetoDesignUSA.com

Cover photograph: Landis Everson

ACKNOWLEDGMENTS

Poems in this collection have appeared in the following periodicals:

The American Poetry Review (2006): "Lemon Tree," "Death Is a Hole," "Hollyhocks," "Mass Destruction," "Landscape with Deer," "Fiction," "In Loving Memory of Norma Carter," "The Sophist"

Barrow Street (2006): "Angel"

Boston Review (2006): "Border Crossings"

Chicago Review (2005): "Jack Spicer in Berkeley: 1949"

Fence (2005): "The Deserted Village"

Fulcrum (2004, 2005): "Postcard from Eden," "The Little Ghosts I Played With," "Hang Up," "Poem from a Line by Robin Blaser," "Genie," "Before Christmas," "Madrigal," "End Game," "Closet," "Elizabethan Moon Song," "How to Remain Dry When It Rains," "A Poem without a Question Mark in It," "I Do the Best I Can," "The Red Wheelbarrow," "A God," "Sentencing"

Harvard Review (2005): "I Reach for My Knight"

Jacket Magazine (2004, 2005): "Where Truth Lies," "At the Window," "Lost Cabin Fire," "Old Rain," "The Sheer Mass of Mass," "Woof," selections from "Postcard from Eden," selections from "The Little Ghosts I Played With"

The Kenyon Review (1958): "Tiger Watch," "Diamonds in Summery Cities," "Angels who have suffered the first forlornment"

LIT (2005): "A Poem That Starts Out Wrong"

Locus Solus (1962): selections from "The Little Ghosts I Played With"

London Review of Books (2006): "Poet's Pepper Tree," "Cassini in Heaven"

The New Republic (2005): "Coronado Poet"

The New Yorker (2006): "On the Terrace"

PN Review (2005): "End Game," "Closet," "Madrigal," "The Red Wheelbarrow," "Poem from a Line by Robin Blaser," "Genie"

Poetry (1955, 1956, 2005): "These friends of yours," "Famine," "The Last Marriage," "Music Appreciation"

Rattapallax (2006): "Song for Nothing"

Seneca Review (2005): "Don't Talk to God," "The Onion and the Piano"

Talisman (1956): "From a Renoir Painting"

Van Gogh's Ear (2006): "School for Scandal"

Verse (2006): "Obit Near Bakersfield," "Obit, August 12th," "Decision For Self-Love," "Thoughts on Hansel and Grethel"

Washington Square (2005): "Sacrifice," "A Prism of Birds"

Zeitgeist Improbable (2004): "Time Zone," "At the Window"

Postcard from Eden was published by James Herndon as a mimeograph booklet in San Francisco in 1960, in an edition of a handful of copies intended for private circulation.

"My Favorite Blond(e)" was published as a broadside by Narcissus Press on behalf of the Woodberry Poetry Room, Harvard College Library, April 27, 2006.

Selections from "The Little Ghosts I Played With" were reprinted in *Poetry Calendar 2005* (Alhambra, 2005).

"Jack Spicer in Berkeley: 1949" and "Coronado Poet" were reprinted in *Poetry Calendar 2006* (Alhambra, 2005).

"The Red Wheelbarrow" was reprinted in the *Emily Dickinson International Society Bulletin* (2006).

"Madrigal" was reprinted in *Mirage/Period(ical)* (San Francisco: October 2005).

"Hang Up," "Madrigal," and "A Poem without a Question Mark in It" were reprinted in the *San Luis Obispo Tribune*, November 14, 2005.

"Mass Destruction" was broadcast on Chicago Public Radio, October 7, 2005.

CONTENTS

EVERYTHING PRESERVED

1955–1960

THESE FRIENDS OF YOURS

These friends of yours are hard to understand.
They shatter sense like stained glass likenesses.
Slowly the dumb dawn sounds attempt emergence,
The sun grows pale and loses futurity.

For there were artificial troubadors
In brilliant colors imitated birds'
Songs, as if the birds sing ravishing
Accurate tunes of all humanity.

Sweet combination of the wise and frail,
These friends of yours want something in their walk.
Awkward, breaking chrysalis of the step,
The limping measure of the heart's adjustment.

Under these heavens of pure, deceitful force
It was forbidden that towers merge or words
With spirit, or heavy souls merge and have
The single sensitivity of wings.

These friends of yours have eyes I cannot watch.
The wrong side of the jewel or prism eats
The hard light and concentrates the vision there.
The colder jewels are hot with most reflection.

For there were troubadors in ancient France
Looked allegorically at men for birds'
Sight, as if the birds fly magically
Within the breast of all humanity.

These friends of yours are hard to understand.
They come and go angelically on glass.
How would the minstrels of Provence paint words
To hide the transmutation of such flight?

FAMINE

In the middle of the night at least twenty deer
Came out upon my pillow to graze,
Gazing down at me with sad, round eyes,
Their pointed hooves quilting my pillow.

And I thrashed gently in sleeplessness,
Moving not to disturb them, wondering
At the famine this year that forces so many
To roam to poor, unfamiliar pastures.

The moon through the window throws cold light
Upon their curved backs, making a forest
Of crossed antler shadows on sheets
That until now have been flawless and starved.

THE LAST MARRIAGE

For one or both, coverlets of peacocks;
In his eyes and hers that wasteful daze;
Their fathers gilt the illustrated dragons,
Their mothers scarcely wept when they conceived.
For so the passage of their days at learning
Has numbed the lashless eyes with calligraphy,
That who has strength to waken first with heartache
And who will thicken first with imagery?

For here is the end of action, like vibration,
A tended trail beyond a crescent bridge,
Where a sleeping time has done away with armies
And peacocks by the hundreds doze in heaps
To hear the duet of that Asian couple—
Long-sleeved and listless by the willow tree—
Awaken all the ancient words for longing:
For an epic battle hymn of preservation
A zither he picks, and she is doomed with song.

FROM A RENOIR PAINTING

On the field she runs, one feels her eyes grow frantic,
Because of so many poppies, or so much distance:
But red no longer hides—she is encircled
And runs that quickly more into the poppies.

This is the dress she wears, russet and common,
Sewn by machine and sold to many ladies;
But not a thread is out of place in poppies.
Her arms are spread to balance her in motion.

Imagine the tiny feet both cruelly crushing
The waxen, heavy blossoms of the poppy.
The path behind her sags and weeps with odor;
The lady herself can hardly help her flight.

For flesh: white butterflies and waxen petals,
The slick grass blades and also her face of fever.
The poppies themselves have no evil intent in growing,
But will they engulf the lady, should she rest?

TIGER WATCH

As a tiger stirs in all his cool ambitions
We have reason to envy and seek the animal.
As the blood paws of the active man strike down
We are the tiger flashing through his kill.

Let there be parables of those who won the cities
Padding upon the streets they built and dying.
There is depravity upon the lamb-like people
Whose hearts are deep in wool, whose wits are dull.

The cries of lambs are like the cry of chaos
Ringing through the hills in lost concern,
Calling forth the tiger to a fatness—
To paw their bodies with a tiger's skill.

Grandeur is handed down in wool-soft language;
Snatches of antique roars still shake the world
From the tiger-watch which sped forth on the lambkins:
Thus Martel, Sobieski; thus Christ's deliberate kill.

DIAMONDS IN SUMMERY CITIES

That all might break to rainbows and a blaze,
For eyes made soft—such city daffodils—
Flounced and parading, these girls twist parasols
Over the sidewalks; girls whose laughter lies
Not in sounds, but in colors, and with colors amuse.

Before them the streets shimmer with pleasurable songs:
Such calico dogs and gingerbread men abound.
Time puts them in a carriage and youth curls near,
The sun and the trees revive, the pigeons multiply—
Such is the world of color one finds here.

Pain turns sleepily in a toy bed. On fine days one sees
Expensive nurses pushing plush baby carriages
Before the Plaza, and horse carriages, and doormen,
And canopies and doll-like limousines.
Therefore, girls reach out stars and make a wish.

A man jumps from a window, the policeman shrills,
The newsstands crackle and the buildings rasp the air.
Boats are sunk in the lake, and a bright red doll
Shrieks "Mama" with hard round eyes; the winds smile twice,
As doubling in their false carriage, girls flash by.

ANGELS WHO HAVE SUFFERED
THE FIRST FORLORNMENT

Angels who have suffered the first forlornment, who now
Lifts up your saddened wings to send you soaring?
O how the mountains thrust up high beyond you,
And how the ocean curls its waves about you!

Angels, awaiting his old command to be forgiven,
Lift up your gentle wings for fresh hosannas.
But how the sharp hills grow up high beyond you,
And how the winds blow down to the very heart.

Humility burns, and banishment is eternal; he said,
Too much hope within us makes us die.
And the mountains use up the heavens all around you,
And the winds and waves are crying, to confuse you.

And this is falsehood, Angels, should he call you; but fold
Your remorseful wings and gently forget his love.
For the mountains are there now, very far above you,
And the winds disperse your godhood everywhere.

POSTCARD FROM EDEN

1.

The calm of the second day, dear Adam, and you might surprise me
Once again with your naked body a white sheet
Against this all-green valley, your detailed stomach
Etched just by breathing. I turn over
Once again with your naked body fixed in my
Memory, here in the fertile valley.

2.

"Get into the motor car!" Have we come of age?
The wheels turn and mama leans back
Eating a banana, her fox
Frizzled about her ears. Ah, how elegant she is
In her limousine, a queen floating above the pavement.
And what's to be said for me at seven, rolling above
The world with her? Shall I too
Eat a banana and share the commanding stare?

3.

Fat Back was a grizzly at the zoo,
Could stand a head and a half above
Any bear there. He begged for junk,
However, and the crowd stood about throwing
Junk at Fat Back day after day
Because he stood so tall and proud.

4.

Each native grinned down at me, white teeth,
Black faces. "Come," I said, "We can be friends."

But they jabbed at me with pink fingers,
Played lovingly with my hair, caressed
My arms and my toes and stared
Excitedly at my eyes.
                              Later I thought
It was a kind of feast, a rather daring,
Elegant party that I'd attended but somehow missed,
Being too careful of certain graces,
Fastidious to oblivion,
Unappreciative, stupid and unaware
Of the delicacies offered anyone there.

    5.

The birds swoop nearer. They are gulls. Why, then,
We must be close to the ocean! Indeed,
The sounds of your music come clearly,
Composing themselves in the air. It was written,
I think, that I'd find you
Against some sort of crazy crashing backdrop
That could go on forever, being an awful bore,
Then change into a storm. But the birds atilt,
Hung in the sky like little notes ranging, the birds
Atilt have no connection with music.

    6.

Enter the store like a millionaire, enter
The door like Adonis. Yes, that lady
Holding the fan means to demand
All she can get. Her husband met me
Behind the drapes where I sat
Drinking stolen cocktails. Yes, that man
Told me the secrets of many a household

With the opening and shutting
Of the fan. Snap, crack, heads tilt back
When I enter the door and the long eyes wait
To stroke me as if the beauty of me
Could be
Pushed out.

7.

The turtle in me
Overcomes me. I am
Easily overcome. He stretches forward
One wrinkled foot, fretfully looks
Up from his snaky neck,
Brings another leg forward and tips
Forward. The turtle in me
Is a sad old thing, overly defensive
And retiring, in a garden of real beauty
Only a curiosity, but subject
To attack.

8.

Evening, evening, why do you wait
To break me? Evening,
Why do you pause? The clowns are too old
For enchantment,
The toys bring tears no longer. Evening—
Like a tree you travel up fiercely,
And burst in little thin leaves
And you wait
Over the ground, casting shadows,
And you wait, evening, casting your shadow all day.

9.

Proceed with the case which makes us face the future.
The ledger looks empty
The ground not covered
As if a cold winter without animals stretched far away.
The naked tree seems hideous
The lines of the register are bare
The courtroom is quiet with disagreeing ghosts
Gesturing. Proceed. Sir, I am young and ugly.
Sir, I am lonely. Sir, who are we?

10.

What a magical uprising of birds! First dead
Snow, then color and a frightened flushed cloud
Of wings clearing the ground! They are scared
But beautiful in fright.
                              And a squirrel takes my gifts.
See! He shakes the leaves to life.
                              So that I knew you in a twice
When I saw you.

11.

The drummer boy beats empty air to life
In rhythm to the fife. The fifer breathes
The air to life. The air begins to mean
With singing, shouts and whispers
And all the hungry senses
Wait to hear your message,
The love in your voice out marching.
The hungry mind is shouting
The words in the empty ear.

12.

Dear Adam, I have been reading Blake all day.
Little Lamb, who made thee?
I am writing to you from the Garden of Eden
Sometime on the second day,
By the stream and over the mead.
This is indeed a place of creation,
A green valley where thoughts can be framed,
As you may remember.

He became a little child. Dear Lamb,
I have been reading Blake to remind me
That when the honey bee has finished a flower
Nothing is really ended. Sweetness and beauty
Surround me, as you may remember.

I'm under the third tree to the left on the face
Of this card. I'm sure you'll remember.
Overhead a new bird is *making all the vales rejoice.*
I say, *we are called by his name.* A shameful
Way to interpret Blake? But then, some sweet ache,
Your ghost under my rib, dear Adam, leaves me no choice.

THE LITTLE GHOSTS I PLAYED WITH

1.

Twilight, dead light, fire light,
Kindling time. The ghost walks.
A mammoth. Afraid of fire? In
Dry light, a new light,
The ghost walks. A snake.
Will it bite? The fear of night
Wakes him. Wet with fear. The snake might
Break the circle, the mammoth
The fire ring. But the moon opens
The lid, lifts over the mountain.

On the seventh day he completed his trek
And came down over the mountain:
Afar south, a flat beach, a tame
Sweet coastline. And that night,
The waves picking up his fire and
Walking it out to meet the moon,
A ghost came to him.
A sign. An ending. A rest. A beginning. The ghost talking.

2.

At the theatre we sit down,
Watch a passion play or farce,
Expect the ghosts to act like us. They review
Things we forgot we knew.

This one is said to be the finest actress of them all. She shows how
Goodness might have discarded us.

Once the play is over, these ghost actors help to deflate
Our feelings, packing them back in the travelling trunk
Which accommodates dresses, crucifixes, junk like
False hair, overwear, a chair, a fur, fair but untrue
To reuse, sucking up air. I'm glad that's over!

A ghost play that ghosts played about us. Come on, now!
They might be in love with us. It's an awesome experience
I never get sick of. Sometimes on a good night I cry
Seeing them cry, like I believe in ghosts for awhile, like
What they said about us can be said
By the dead.

3.

The perfect form of woman is a ghost,
A phantom cheap like pathos to dissolve us,
A style-shifting sweetness, a no-no choice
Of basically bad quotations.

She does, however, create a vast holiness,
A kitsch of culture that randomness sorts out,
An excitement like leaves falling to lighten the murk,
A forest forced open to a golden expanse—
And this, yes, I can give thanks for.

"My leaves have fallen from me!" That's ghost
Talk, just the last of the ups and downs.
I don't like people knowing what I'm thinking.
I want more fun years, one iconoclastic notion.
After all, ghosts have been with us forever.

Her love could appear rolled up in a coded raindrop,
Ghostwritten. Anything else is trickery, a goofball excitement.
Those no-strings-attached broken promises you cry so much about
Reading message boards? I told you once before
They were nothing more than a farewell appearance.

4.

The miracle began when no one expected it.
The lights shining now through the trees tell us
The significance of the heightened accidental effect.

Mobs shouted and the bells rang. All through it
Her tears
Flowed
Springlets from the eyes
Of the picture.
                              Her death
Bloomed like little mistakes between the bricks.

When no one wanted it . . .
The people gathered
Her Death wept for their blindness.

The light, such as the light surrounding Her image,
Touches the leaves at our feet
As we walk carefully through these ghosts
The live leaves allow us.

5.

To do what should be done, let us pretend
That nothing's there. At the river's mouth the sweet

Turns salty. An in-between place, no trace, not even a palm tree,
Of what should be there.
                    You will be stared at.
People will smell your skin, hot, but cooling, sweat
Still sweet, a chemical scent. You made it. Boats
Bob up and down. I am inside myself now, floating
On an old fire that no one sees. A staged catastrophe.

I try to describe you to the river. I say you're a snag—
Something the river can understand—catching my heart,
That I'm rowing without oars, that this is some trip,
Never able to leave you, bracing hard against swirls

That confuse me, that the whole ghostly place seems like a trap
Without bait, that nothing arrives anyplace near
Where you and I once wanted to be.

  6.

Solomon said, "We are wed,
Let me do your dancing."
Am I too old to love you?
Am I too young to love you?
Is any time the right time
To love you?

They look full at my face. What are they seeing? That love is not
Just on your face?
Is it on my face, too?
I could quote you forever
You are more beautiful than trees.

7.

Voices come when we listen.
In a little garden

She stops to pick a flower.
She directs the gardener
In his duties. She says,
"Voices come when we listen . . ." to flowers.
. . . Her voice, for instance, like cold fire,
Illuminating her order. We walk
The cultivated garden.

Voices inside her mirror, the reflected
Mouth opening and closing, expression of pain,
Amusement, the face changing
The heart. Speak of a different degree
Of living, as if to prepare for marriage.

8.

In the distance a rose tree is like a cloud
Seeded with red roses. It's actually bleeding
A shower of pain. All day a blue yesterday fell falling—
At least that's the way she sees it.

She sits there outraged and disgraced,
Her overstocked emptiness bloats her with shame,
A universally serious sign of decay, an embarrassing closet
Reeking with garbage rage. She should be ashamed. The rain

Taps with its feet her opinion of music
Rat-tatting the roof, a recruiting of red notes that

Birds can sing in mutual vibration.
But she's badly out of tune.

A concert-quality conceit makes her color blind and tone deaf,
Her memory of roses is out of date and despondent. She could help it.
But she likes the blues. It's her chilling sense of humor. Oh God!
Look! Someone's dead mud oozes under her shoes!

9.

Now that Santa Claus has left me
What will I do for another?
All the toys lie broken where I threw them.
I play too rough. I don't cherish what I'm given.
I remember his kisses that always forgave me,
Entering my heart like elegant reindeer.

He invented the spirits we always called Christmas, the ghosts
Of things pleasant, so I never felt fearful.
I should have. I made him too strong.
That's why he has now gone. He used to
Let me wander his estate under
The black pines and over the silverdollar lakes.

If the blizzards should overtake me, as they sometimes did,
Coming across me lost and chattering, he hugged me and laughed
And showed me how to walk through snow. That was not
Long ago. Why did he desert me when I smashed
The little ghosts he gave me? They were merely
Toys only, really, they were not real like the reindeer.

10.

A key under the roots
Winds the tree. A present fit
For Heaven. The branches shake
The apples bang together. A chiming tree.

I put it on the stage below the mountain.
I'm going to sell the handsome slave, the one called Adam.
I'm going to sell his suitcase, his gloves, his silver cane,
His underwear, his shoes. I'll put him back in Eden.

He's all that's left now of his earthly estate.
I threw away the key that winds the other keys. But nothing stops.
The moon rises anyway. The tree keeps time, the apples
Clocking. The slave, stripped to his stockings

Still waits to be sold. It's time to stop this show, I think,
Or change the apples to lemons. I can do
With a shift of scene and the audience, too, seems tired.
Thing is, nobody wants perpetual emotion. Jack told me

"Nothing happens unless you make it happen." He only meant
The opposite of love was dragging him down, his heart
Too angry for a loss he never had. That wasn't hate,

Though it kept on going. It's getting late now and
Nothing's sold, nothing wound down, nothing stopped at all.
And our love for our ghosts exhausts us.

11.

If you're not born of woman,
You're a confection on a sour day, a sweet kid

With good teeth and a skull of love that never
Never knew a sin. Eyes look out of you,
Innocent but delighted.

Within, though knowing your ghost is holy,
You would swap an alligator on a bet
If your flesh could touch flesh and, oh yes,
Not only that, but Glory would not stop
Screaming and screaming about love.

Look around the ground for a sermon,
Something to take your mind off your dreaming.
Keep yourself uptight and for God's sake stop scheming!
"Amen," said the man who first sold real estate.
"The desert is purest because it lacks water."

12.

A high heart. Ah! What has it climbed to?
Never the purple, the blue of altitude
That we aren't chilled and smothered; the heart, too.
See here that you have five fingers, each one
A curling tool? Then have you annexed the hand?
The high heart is smothered.
Without the leg, the lip, the genital
There is no important movement, but a gasping.

Lyoncorda blew a trumpet when I was young.
The hills in their high crowns held the sounds.
The valley departed from the birds and brush, became
A smooth cup of trees, featureless.
By the blowing all was stilled and I afraid

That such a small thing, a human girl,
Could dumb nature. I was transformed

By a power beyond the horn, I rode
Away from her singleness as in fear from the cold.

13.

Independent and in her grace I grant
Much of me that no other commands. A horse
Gift, a true ivory, a small seed of selflessness,
A wind over the high plain. I remain

A knight, if you wish, an armored lover,
Delicate and deadly. Think as you will.
The wind is insane, truly, not the stiff stick
That ends fluttering overhead. Her flag.

14.

"It is as much a breach of promise to love
That way, as if you had promised not to love."

I said that remembering
The holy vows I meant.

Two doves I have.
I twist their necks. One I eat,
The other I should throw
Far away.

Because love is raw and rots instantly
I protect you from
That frail fulfillment
So your damned ghost won't flicker
Into the far corners
                          on and on

Until it blows up or burns out,
Wanting burning.

2003-2005

HANG UP

The telephone Jean Harlow picked up
and slammed down three times in 1935
made the cock crow in our heads. The ringing
went on long after we fell asleep
in our beds. I swear
my heart beat faster on a long-dead mattress.
There's still a chance
another day after
that I can be on the other end of a line,
someone worthy enough for her
to hang up on
on a dime.

POEM FROM A LINE BY ROBIN BLASER

"A pool played with its ripples"

Did you think I would steal your poem?
I went down to the pool to look at it
Fragile, pretty
You didn't need me
The ripples spoke
They broke my heart
This is what the ripples said
"I love you"

That's what I wanted the poem to say
Or the pool
Or at least the ripples, saying
"It's OK to steal my poem"
You always forgave me
A line by you
Never did need me.

I could shout out your name over the pool
That plays with its meanings. The meanings are ripples that
Hear but don't listen
That love, but the ear
Listens to water.

GENIE

The poem grows
a preconceived experiment
the lab scientists knew exactly
how at the end
the test tube would turn blue.

But, bam!
a bright explosion
an experiment gone odd.
Out of the disaster a genie scowls.
A bridge collapsing
the engineer swore it would hold
3 elephants at one time
but one, only one
cracked the suspension.

The elephant fell into the river.
It was the end of the bridge, the circus and the waterlilies,
but the best thing that happened,
the genie unfolded.
Give a free poem to each poet who promises us
an early death.

I REACH FOR MY KNIGHT

To start the game, reach
for the knight who moves magnificently down to us
from the far-off dimension of heroes. Abstract
and concrete detain us, take up space
that spirits might inhabit. Victory is a
primitive corruption of love. Victory
is a prehensile idea in Dawn forests dead
long before Diana of the handsome bow
was invented. If the Bishop shows up,
eyes dancing with fury, kill him at first sight
with stones. He is no hero but an afterthought
and sorrow rides his robes. He works for his king.

Echoes and scolding are his messages and he prays for gain.
Instead, play me the game again, but not to win, play
on a flat plain with the knight on it alone
naked except for the fine horse and
that long lance stretched forth into the future
and the Holy Grail he's always searching for
that is said not to exist—
I will hold that under my ribs where life itself begins.

JACK SPICER IN BERKELEY: 1949

He was in Berkeley under an
umbrella of rain
watching a rolling ballgame
wearing a raincoat in the dry season
with no umbrella for shelter
because he ignored the weather
and his words lacked rain. His words
lacked sun. They were birds
in search of each other,
like a pinball machine in action,
like spyglasses magnifying jokes, mere
suggestions of hope.

He was in Berkeley making it real
among the shadowy, quick-moving statues
on their way to classes to listen to lectures
by ghosts who had lost hope
in the Second Coming of Ghosts.
He was shabby because he knew
elegance was poetry in disguise.
He liked masks and alchemy, finally
looking that way, moving across his memory
to rewrite it under the pressure
of ghosts who were slow to arrive.

He was in Berkeley on his way to Ghostland.
He was pissed off he wasn't there.
He liked both kinds of joys
but couldn't choose between them.
He didn't know he was crossing town to invent,
despite the traffic in the streets

and the virginity of his sheets,
poetry no one else had seen.
He believed in *La Bonne Fée*—
the Good Fairy—but he never found him.

DEATH IS A HOLE

Death is a hole, or a gap
in the hole. The radio talks Texan,
the plain outside is shabby.

A false desert lost in its own dream.
I think of the forsaken rabbits, hope
they come back to me. I was a sex slave

near Tecate in the Casa Grande Hotel
spread-legged on the dining room table
the man called me Mable

no rabbits were available. Insanity
not an option, was not a remedy anyway
but the song down the throat

of death did sound beautiful, like rain
over a dry place sucking for air as with
a knife in my teeth I descend the stair.

It was a border town called Gates of Hell.
You know it, too? Filled with rabbits that
forsake you when you need them the most.

They were bygone days that should not have come
on a phantom planet that death controlled
always around, damn it, like static on the radio.

HOLLYHOCKS

Why weren't they arranged alphabetically,
the hollyhocks, too? Ungainly Gulliver
bloomed in a small garden; the queen
admired the forbidden view
as her coach rolled under his spread legs
while the king acted in a kingly way
before thousands cheering the parade.

Gulliver was a hollyhock
with a cock too big
for any woman in town. The
flower of the kingdom
too gigantic for picking.
All the little people cheered,
they knew what for,
and always hollyhocks
have been too large for
the small flowers. You can't
alphabetize it, not since
those forbidden fruits fell around our heads
like Bibles instead of dictionaries.

Love is forever up
too high in the branches to reach
and too disorganized to fit together
once you get down to it, like Aesop
mixing it up with his own fables.

MASS DESTRUCTION

I would like to go through
a country full of people,
not looking for what I'm
not looking for. About Lewis Carroll,
even the Rabbit had an important date,
something about reality or fate—
I think he had no idea what for,
except to have forever something important
in store. This much is true, we don't find
what we're looking for. It's the search.

Usually we make it our business
to invent rabbit holes,
"gathering threats" as opportunities arise.
The Rabbit looks at his watch:
"Gotta get outta here." A dream, from here to there.
"Gotta get to where
I am seeing myself someplace else." What am I
not looking for?
Even the Looking Glass demanded evidence.

The door opened on self destruct.
People were dying and there were tanks.
I can't keep redreaming a dream that went bust.
The Rabbit holds a watch but never has time.
I feel like Alice. Everything surrounds me
in a trance of not looking.

LEMON TREE

A tree that grew in the Garden of Eden
a tree of innocence called
the Tree of Good and Evil. It was harmless

as opposites are in balance. It was also
tasteless,
the taste of innocence before it is betrayed.
When God removed the wall

he gave the lemon thorns and bitterness because it had
no hostility.
It is a taste we want most to subdue. It asks
to be left alone.
We use it with fish and tea. We sugar it.

Look out the window. It stands with a donkey's
stance, hoping the day will pass.
Its scent through the curtains
cuts through
mustiness, sharp
with sweet blossoms. It hides the smell
of new babies.

ANGEL

The Lost and Found lady—
talk to her. She's not sympathetic.
"I haven't had a honeymoon in 3 years," she says.
What is she talking about? What does she mean?

If you ask her if they left your wings
she doesn't care. She won't even look through
that pile of feathers in the room's corner.
She fixes her lipstick. She doesn't tell you

the way to Niagara Falls or the Grand Canyon.
She wants you to get lost. If you lead her on,
tell her she's beautiful hoping she'll look for your

wings, she's on to you, she'll make no effort to help you.
Put on your sorrowful look and take off.
She'll look in the mirror and pat her hair.
You'll lose more than wings if you stay.
You'll lose your way
of dancing on a pin.

TOM SWIFT AND HIS GIANT LOSS

Without much fanfare or irony
I roll the giant cannon forward,
maybe tightrope walkers or common clowns
will defy death and die anyway before it.

My mouth, too, is big and loud.
All the cannibals in the zoo can't hold it
or the trick riders in the carnival
stay afloat on my ringtossed hopes.

Without much of a fan or a single fare
a bankrupt zoo comes tumbling down.
All I used to think were clever tricks
are blown out fuses and refusals.

WHERE TRUTH LIES

The truth of your lies
renames me. I am not a name.
The street is swept of leaves.
Homeless dogs invade the park.
My own backyard could not be
more beautiful
than the shadows of difference
between what you say
and the escape of shadows
behind words.

Sun and shade.
Truth that I am loved.
People say the watchdog
will never bite
unless silence fills him.
True, I am not loved.

Listen to what you're saying.
Watch the shadow.
It covers your mouth.
Who taught you to open your mouth

against the caress of a
rough shadow?
I can't imagine a tongue
without a mouth to lie in.
Lying in your mouth.

MUSIC APPRECIATION

The violin plays with the tide
coming in,
with water rushing over sand,
a hand held over power.
The sea bows back.
It is a musical interaction, an intersection of

waves up, waves down and up. Love rubs like
wet seaweed over rocks.
This goes on until a resemblance grows
between the chin and the violin.
Where they scrape
something else takes their place, a

sitting-in of
deep-sea gravity
or perhaps an undertow,
a pulling-me-out-through-the-ears.

Music could be a tuba pretending to be
a tall tree talking to itself about wind

or the crash of cymbals and drums
imitating tables
that reach the seabeds with their legs.

Always the same scale.
In the mornings our longings dress up
for love. First they take a quick dip
of deep resentment.

DECISION FOR SELF-LOVE

Sometimes you write poetry about poetry.
You can't help yourself.
Your fingers stray down there where there is
still feeling

left over from childhood,
like sucking your thumb.
The poem gets closer to your way
of doing business.

On the chest of drawers the teddy bear
someone's mother put there
doesn't crack a smile
as you leave it out.

MADRIGAL

The flavor of the pudding sits in its cup
remembering itself. It's all it has to do,
and be eaten. I came into your room. You had
the globe of the world next to your bed.

"Do you want pudding?" You spun the world like a spider's web
with your finger, not even asking what flavor.
I held the cup close to my heart.
All I had to do by myself was
eat it up.

SURFER

They say, "Surf's up!"
How many waves to make such a simple statement?
How many surfs beforehand?

and hands on the board standing up, something
not even the waves had thought of,
riding water upside down into the land.

Balance against smashup, keeping the mortal faith.
   Water nymphs
haven't the means
to average out the waves. These are real people dying,
not dice. Have no way
to understand jelly fish
the gambol of love against love
white combers that can tear us apart

falling on Neptune's toes
miles from the planet Mars or the gods
of yore. Pardons galore. Indifference makes its
immortal war against joy,
if you roll.
There are never two waves alike. Surf always changes
by bedtime.

CASSINI IN HEAVEN

The robotic Global Martian Surveyor
seeing a dozen circular craters
landed in a depression, in dust, forgot

stored orders. A cold beauty looking for ghosts
within range, looking for another us on a planet raw,
a really different kind of orbit to operate through

layers, which are wrapped in a "harmonious symphony."
"Queen Mary will host a major space conference," her crown
realized in "sunlight from the upper left." A thin

wind, but no windmills. No moon named Triste. This
is the way onions act, peeling layers and wobbling.
Cassini saw a halo of moons, Saturn's metaphorically-

layered rings, not unlike a pearl necklace whirling
heartlessly, tearlessly, cut into rock, drilling
down to the ring-spinning pearl beauty. "Pearl onions,"

and I laughed, rich nitrogen and hydrocarbons, the bright
storm of the swirls and eddies near Phoebe's lifeless
dark material. Wouldn't it be another laugh if the

metaphor exploded our whole Theory of Innocence?
The mechanical tears gravitate into real moons.
"There's something I have to tell you," one of the

astronauts whispered, forgetting we were listening. The President
a vast void beyond our concept of good and evil, the
sun a hot dot, dead dustballs. So, not everything reflects love.

AT THE WINDOW

Insanity is a precious thing under
an umbrella and grows like twisted vines
in our heads. Sometimes the rain comes down

to tickle us and drown out our tears.
The cows outside the institution
have none of our fears. At the window

the bars seem to shift shadows
on the backs of the sweet beasts, and
I wonder at the pastures of peaceful stupidity

that are always inside them to eat.
Like zebras one moment, if the sun
is just right with the bars, their made-up

stripes dance, until the rains come
to put them out. I wonder why
these magic drops tickle when they don't

hit me on the ears and like crinkled paper
getting wet, the vines uncurl and grow straight
until the rain stops and waits for the zebras.

OBIT NEAR BAKERSFIELD

John Robinson's wife's sister born
in a recent issue of Newsweek
of a Presbyterian minister
near Douglas County
linked to his brother
on October 14, 1903

disclosed that cracks in the corners
caused her sister Martha to settle.
The main building collapsed of window openings.
She grew and made use of the church
"For reasons of my Father's health."
After the marriage
the beautiful kerosene lamps
perhaps by her fifth child
burned until her retirement.
Those who attended her funeral found

little damage done by homesteading
before with no electricity
before the earthquake, though
before water seepage was strong.
Still, more and more people moved away
despite her survival by children.

WORD PLAY

You worship the fine tuning
most of all,
the sight of your own words
purring before you,
how they weave in and out of meaning,
pushing like cars in and out of traffic, the idea
being to beat the odds,
the other guy, get there first.

I don't see why the rush,
the cleverness, when the highway
retraces itself,
keeps going all around the world,
a huge circle never reaching the stars,
words cutting in and out
of each other
till naturally by the law of averages
you'll have a horrible wreck,
an accident,

becoming the only way to end the poem—
headlights screaming in your eyes,
hands up to protect your soul,
the steering wheel inside your heart
killing the thing you most adored—
ultimately a bad driver hung out
under the stars, or unwittingly,
tangled in the wreck
of somebody else's poetry.

LOST CABIN FIRE

The National Weather Service calls
for isolated lightning storms, Oh Lord,
and the threat of fire most honorable,
visible and beautiful in the night.

Not a warrior, a girl or the moon,
but the gift of Prometheus to man,
surprising even the blind spectator
has also burned 421,000 acres.

Called "The Lost Cabin Fire," the crew
said it was burning half the west.
I saw it chewing on the moon, eating it up,
consuming $330,345 to date.

Holding your hand in the low humidity
as if you were part of the fire crew
I prayed for rain but at the same time
the destruction thrilled me out in the wild zone.

OLD RAIN

How can time matter
if a thing once known
such as a language or a god
can be reborn
without derision or shame?

Love in the hotel
where it has stopped before is
in the same worn room.
Stars
older than wisdom itself
make light each night,
a book read
whose chapters repeat and repeat,

or that seen through new tears
old rain walks up and down
in the trees
outside
just around the corner
from what happened before.

SONG FOR NOTHING

So now the sun shines on Raggedy Ann
—JOANNE KYGER

I remember the past
you remember the future
Together you'd think we would couple up
to become rich and famous
lover-seers.

        But the case is cold
the way snails walk at night
leaving their trails as
silver tokens for the morning.
You can see where they were headed
but not where they went or came from.

You can also imagine a moon shining
even if there wasn't a moon,
even if I imagined there was a moon lighting up
the dark sky for us, and you,
instead, could imagine only a dawn,
even if there wasn't a dawn, eclipsed,
with no love in it.

TIME ZONE

Honor me with thanksgiving
on the day of my birth,
that you were born to walk beside me
as strangers on sidewalks and mountainsides.
How holy are the moments that
we share under the same sun,
that we were not created apart
separated by centuries. Even

though you walk as far away as China
while I walk the Andes, even though
beasts surround us now and
not the sons of their deaths,
even though the beds you sleep in
will never hold the life of my love,
the weight of this chance time together
should fill us with gratitude that
time loves the unity of our separate bones.

IN LOVING MEMORY OF NORMA CARTER

I'll take your long legs and
the afterthought of thunderstorms
or sex all day rolled up
against a green bank wet from us
far away. I'll take what I can get

not fight not getting it, nor fight
not wanting it, or not wanting
not getting it, nor when we bathe
in our granite bath, water from our wings
or from our fingers flicker over

the darktown destinies that shudder
grabbing Heaven a second, not settling down
riding it up and down, forms and feathers,
seeing you through jewelry now, soft
coming up behind me, not wanting it maybe.

ON THE TERRACE

The lonely breakfast table starts the day,
an adjustment is made to understand
why the other chair is empty. The morning
beautiful and still to be, should woo me. Yet
the appetite is not shared, lost somewhere in memory.

How lucky the horizon is blue and needs
no handwriting on its emptiness. I am
written on thoroughly, a lost novel
found again. I remember the predictable plot too late,
realize the silly, sad urgency of moss.

BEFORE CHRISTMAS

Almost
the first reindeer
shipped North by boxcar from Lapland
but a toy model
got there first.

A dwarf invented reindeer on his own.
He was Santa's favorite. He
hadn't known
they already existed.

This discouraged dwarf
was close to taking his life but
Santa showed up
encircled by snow.
He said, "I will use the real reindeer for my sled

always in yoke
to your original invention."
That night the gears that turned the Pole
stopped
and began to turn the other way,
so it be so.

My love is a toy model waiting
for a reindeer to carry me.

OBIT, AUGUST 12TH

On August 12th, wearing glasses,
Rosa Belafante passed away
beloved wife and native of
and her collection of goldfish pearls
continued to take care of
that she faithfully served
the kind spirits, gold-encrusted ghosts
that have known her all their deaths,
who enjoyed bowling
in the churchyard and bat hunting
near the Tweechee River Canyon.

A lake that big learned kindness.
Noted some intense blurring at first.
Surrender was her deepest blessing.
Blessed are those high school,
coast guard, jewelers and post office
employees who last beyond
cancellation, where good health, that
failing flag of forgiveness, gave way. Oh,
when Rosa died she took us with her. She haunts
the memory of August 12th, dawned dead this day.

THE DESERTED VILLAGE

The meadow borrows
a glamorous toolbox
because color has not fallen
with the lack of rain.

Glass
breaks to pieces inside my ear
though the houses stand
firm by their windows.

Bravery
is as old as a humbled spirit
and looks me straight in the eye from the living rooms, where
there are cities, too,
in the midst of the village,
locked doors knocked open by the out-of-doors.

SCHOOL FOR SCANDAL

Mary had her little lamb
confused with the Big Bad Wolf.
Long ago, a poem or a pop-up book became so enormous,
childhood was like a house of prostitution
with a lot of elementary patrons
there to get it any way they could.

Rich folks, poor folks
have always been taught a sweettooth for the exotic.
Fairies. Spiders. Plums. Pocket-posies.
Whatever fancy suits us,
we'll stoop down to take it in our mirrors.

Oh, we were so timidly ridiculous
harboring in our hearts the little secrets
we learned so young from
the nursery rhymes
they kept repeating to us over and over
until we had to adjust,
one way or the other.
Tuffets.

THOUGHTS ON HANSEL AND GRETHEL

For Jack Spicer

The duck in the story who saved the kids
is you swimming through your poem,
the only hero in a bitter story
that everyone misses.

Your arms flail up and down
make the sound water makes when it talks
and the deeper you go
the words hurt.

But it's your poem
you swim alone in.
The fish accuse everything, rolling their eyes
the duck swims circles around blue skies.

The radio tossed in as trash long ago still
plays old love songs like new.
Air, water, love—
the vocabulary your words must breathe through.

DON'T TALK TO GOD

I can't hold you responsible for an act of God
which love must be, or birds hatching or
falling down dead, towers knocking themselves over.

I can't open both arms and catch falling towers,
catch trees, catch helpless oceans or drowning things.
I hold out empty arms because you refuse
to fall into them.

Every bit of you inside won't come out,
which is the way of a heart hatching.
This stubbornness insists I love you while I hold
no act of God responsible.

I guess love first requires empty arms
with a sun between them
before clouds start to fill spaces
before songs start before even the trees.

SACRIFICE

First, the lamb I never sent you.
The forest. The wolves. Even
the postman with his sack of mail. Trapped, our
answers to each other eaten up.

I can't love you if the mailman and the lamb are eaten up.
My letters are beginning to resemble love.
Lost   undelivered
No return address
kissed shut.

My teeth are ground down to kisses.
Harmless.
I wanted to mail you a lamb—
innocence you could kill with kisses.

But all the eaten mailmen quit trying.
The forest snarled with echoes.
Once upon a time in a nasty forest
I ate the last lamb myself
to cheat the wolves
because your stamped envelopes stayed unanswered.

A postman said, "But the wolves ran off
        a long time ago."

Fall was coming.
I ripped off my clothes left and right to dance
until my bones woke up to realize they were poems.
Trembling, the trees began to undress, too.

Darlings, innocent of amber,
watching their own beautiful poems follow the postman.

1. Who is the real hero of this poem? 2. Do the wolves represent winter, jealousy, other wolves or disguises? 3. Why is Little Red Riding Hood not in the poem? 4. Is the Post Office in the forest, in another poem or in a misplaced box? 5. Are the trees in love with the mailmen, each other or mirror images? 6. Why are echoes like envelopes? 7. Would you sign your name to this poem? 8. Not everything is asked in a question? Some footnotes are always incomplete? Like history? dictionaries and poems?

A POEM THAT STARTS OUT WRONG

Put nothing down to distress the reader.
No barking dog.
No rustle in the place whispers belong
or photos of petals near collapse.
Erase oranges of confusing taste, a face
wrinkled or in pain,
a map with waterless rivers or water
without a bend,
still in darkness. Here, where mystery

beyond hope comes too near,
make a bright flight of leaves
descend, none to smear all our spotless
rivers. A map folds and unfolds, does not
bunch or wrinkle. Rainbows to last.
The First Endlessness of Eden.
This was the spot I was to start on, a leg
steps out of the lake,
a step falters instead into dashes that spread without prints onto the
    screaming bank.

END GAME

Do you believe the story of the airline pilot
who got lost in the fog
(his first date in two years)
on the streets of England
and fell into real water and drowned?

Did you believe the story of the little girl
who got lost in the streets of London
stopped a notoriously greedy and stingy
taxidriver to drive her home
got the ride and made a penny.

Do you believe the story of the millionaire
who knocked on your door
and asked you to pick out of a list
the true story of loss
where there was none?

That small mice underfoot
tell these stories only
they aren't really mice they are aliens
looking like mice
and their purpose is never discovered.

Then why do you go to the lengths you do
to write small poems about great episodes
and big poems about nothing
if there's a rush
to capture the castle of the king?

LANDSCAPE WITH DEER

The forest I step in has to be imaginary.
Can you imagine me following you otherwise,
me a non-trail blazer? Even the deer
large-eyed, tawny with twitching tails
were misplaced from the zoo. Do you

wonder, when you hear the mountains
in my speech that I'll never penetrate those trees
because they have become real to me,
and why I shake so in retreat
fearing the snowdrifts, the avalanches, the
broken landscapes that have made you unreachable, a fable to tell
    to deer
before they learn old ways to be wild.

CLOSET

It doesn't need to be
important.
It doesn't need to be.
The door
doesn't need to open.
The door
doesn't need to be.

I see
the stars right through the back
of your head.
They talk to me
as if you were not a closed contentment.
I hear music
where you are inside talking to tomorrow,
a blinking of night and day
where you remember.

All the toys I gave you
for every reason
fall out of the closet where
the door
is a single bird passing beyond a flower.

FICTION

Compose
alongside a row of punctuation marks
laid open
invented for our breath for
our ways of loving.
Isn't it like that, the rows
of houses scattered over rock and dirt,
poetry, music, art,

the true flames
built on and edged with lawns,
cobblestones, asphalt, sand, leaves.
I look at you,
it could be over a fence where your laundry
hangs or spins in the basement alone.

We are cleaning up our Acts, our Revelations our Genesis.
We are looking into eyes
that would breathe in deeply if they had
lungs and involuntary
otherwise outraged heartbeats.

THE SHEER MASS OF MASS

Available in whale, elephant, suede shoes and fleas
depending on the bulk of the observer
the position of the Constellations, the color
of whatever color or sigh that happens by.
I would love to wrap myself safe in miasma.

Weight and heft and obscurity are not
able to walk under umbrellas or size up the days.
There is a lurch in space to accommodate
the tiny moon rising for the night.
Royal heron land ponderously on a pond.
Laughter heard through the earplugs of the gods.

ELIZABETHAN MOON SONG

Sleep comes downstairs in a jasmine mist
rubbing its arms and the top of its head.
There are lights on in the livingroom
and the clock shows an early morning hour.

A rush of love as soft as my slippers
drives sleep from my heart. Here among furniture
I see the moon has been ignored
because Julia left the lights on, forgetful.

We musn't forget to put things right,
turn off what isn't needed to turn on what is.
One can eclipse love by mistaking
the forgetfulness of Julia for the moon.

HOW TO REMAIN DRY WHEN IT RAINS

Closed in my arms there have been flowers
or a stranger on a twilight bed
guns and white packages and the long
odd sadness of my lover's face.

Most curious of all have been the poems
holding me wide as they left my house
allowing in shouts from the strange streets
of trouble or joy or the death of secrecy.

I carry a map case full of scenarios
because like sand it can give me traction
when words from another intention ask to come in
and the dictionary yells out they are liars.

THE SOPHIST

"And when we call him a maker of images
he will ask us what we call an image."
I'll say, the Funny Papers in the 30s were
when the sun had real rays like fat crayon lines.
The hero's Adam's apple was a mystery. He wore rags
and had a dog who talked philosophy.

We are blessed in the rays of the sun.
Look what we dreamed up!
Eyes wide
and the little dog digs a hole in the page.
Not even the pet rabbits were so real.
What I call an image

is what I made in school out of clay.
Fifty times I bowed down to what I made
mad joy, pride, indifference
and lots more sins came into me.
Put the clay thing on the funny page with the dog—
there are impatient idols along my ten fingers.

SELF-TAUGHT

The perfect piano lesson on a stool of water
is a single cut flower arranged in 88 vases.
The notes press trembling into deep white ponds
while a selfish geography kills the dried tambourines.

The piano lesson is a clean door through a sky
absolutely without imperfection, an exercise hinged on
clouds, stars, rain, doves and mirrors open to variation.
There is a sliding scale of angels created

starkly for angels, fingertips humming, kissing, picking through
    their bright keys.
A big bang of chords echoes off the groin's memories.
The hands must be clean, to let the mysteries correspond,
each solution carved and gilded before it is gone.

The last notes of the piano lesson beg you to step aside—
the rest of the lesson needs to get by. It's summer.
Only a perfect recital is allowed the run of the Garden
where the Gardener weeds out the deafness of his flowers.

CORONADO POET

I am an old man who writes like the 40s.
My suntan is a period piece.
Young men then spent all day at the beach
to avoid reality.
                                    I stay upright.
Nothing makes me go down dusty roads to change my style.
I don't believe in love anymore, the foghorn
blasted it out of me.
                          Jack Noble
died of skin cancer, his life cooked out on the sand . . .
in his coffin waves will break.
Between his knees sandcastles fight back.
How many bathing suits did he wear out
in 70 years?

Among the valleys of the distant waves
we will eventually meet. Hi Jack, I'll say.
Well it won't matter who got the superior tan.
The orange sun will recognize us. It owes us.

It will be the sun from nineteen hundred and forty-forever.
O no cloud in the sky! O ocean full of fish hiding!
The sun seduced us before we could be virgins.

A POEM WITHOUT A QUESTION MARK IN IT

Do you abhor desire
when you see it in the mirror
missing its clothes
moving nearer.
Are you afraid

of the tables filled with food
that your mood
might shift
and you might not want to eat a
meat, fruit, potato or sweet

because of the great emptiness
watching around you.
If there appeared a stranger to you
bending down for a kiss
unexpectedly

would you walk without clothes
out of the mirror's view
to discover if it is you who
are the true stranger
you promised yourself to.

Does your face open on hinges
and inside two strangers entwine
and a trumpet sings out each time you look out
of the space left out
when your eyes shine in.

I DO THE BEST I CAN

"I do the best I can." Words of defiance.
Words of defeat. Smiling against the car we built together.
After the wreck, wheels upside down, still turning.
In the distance, sirens yell themselves closer.

The sirens try to come to our rescue. Still a love song
wailing in the heart. It already lures us the wrong way
to Oklahoma. The pull so great it could have been
Okinawa or Oceanside. Why have the roads become dead

ends, circles, fairy tales, banjo songs, clothespins, love itself?
"Polar bears also face extinction"—(yet their numbers grow
like auto wrecks) "I could meet you at the Pole." You could be
on top of our smashup, smiling for reporters, slowly,

like icebergs and love, dissolving into the paleolithic waters where
    love began.

A GOD

You aren't the only ones who have been out there
and come back. Lyons and zephyrs and dead flower arrangements
climb up the trellys to reach Heaven and
fail. Fall right at my feet and stay there.

My slippers were once owned by Ozma or I forget
the Wicked Witch of the West, but the wind changes
like kings and baseball teams. Now outside
what we used to call the Gates of Hell

all the good people who were once bad
line up like angels to change back to
whatever they thought they should have been,
while I walk among them, a god in red slippers.

THE RED WHEELBARROW

Shocking, the red wheelbarrow there,
the cheerless sight of it
reproachful,
made for an October need. It never
wanted me. Piled with dried beanstalks.

Rusting in the sun, waterlogged and tired.
Did the idea of it die in my hands once,
as we struggled together over the fake furrows, me
with no plan for love, the wheelbarrow sobbing?

Trying to be whole, grow leaves again,
touch the air. Our needs
were different, transitory. I saw birds scavenging the fields, while
the wheelbarrow rotted in my arms.

The moon is up for grabs. Nothing
I make wants it.

4 PARTS UPON A GROUND

I'm sitting around a table. I have divided myself
magically
into four hearts
to entice a lost bird
to fly into a poem for lost poetry.
In medias res. A novelty I have never constructed.

In from the condensation of centuries
a rare beast
begins to graze in my meadow. All of me
must note the press of its hooves on old grass,
its nobility.
No bird's print. An animal from Eden.

Looking for a bird and finding a beast Adam never named.
The ability
to agree that we see the same moment, watch
what is and isn't. Write it down with one pen,
quickly. It steals my eyes where a bird should be.

A WALTZ FOR TRUMPETS

Harsh notes jump into the sea,
this waltz wants to swing. Nothing like it
ever blew off the highly polished midnight waters.
One, two, three, one, two, three
try to break free as the trumpet screams
into the ballroom sky.
                              Pick your feet up
and start to hop. How many times
you been this far down? Dry skirts
shake up the place, face set from hot prancing
off the waxed floor of ballroom dancing.

It's time to move away from the moon, get around,
the Devil will tell you the place to die,
curtains open over the window to Hell.
A fast car is driving under the sea,
stopping to open the door, lady you get in
wet through from a dance forbidden to trumpets,
lady get in before the notes learn to drown.

SHOPPING WITH SAPPHO

I'm avoiding the radio of hate, whose side I'm on.
The dial is stuck on junk. A selection
of jams and jellies runs up and down the market
shelves, so I don't listen. My hands
reach for the sweets
three times.

I decide not to buy Orange Of Macanaria,
Blueberry Of Flosse or the most exotic
"Nectar Of Zeus" label, although
a disembodied static asks my hand
what does my belly crave that is not my loins?

Having so long ago forgotten the pure path
alongside the Alpheus
(or was it Rio Mame or the River Santee?)
where can I find desires equal in worth
to the essences tight in these jars?

One atop another they could touch the intentions
of Olympus
where even the poorest goddess, bending low,
can clearly buy what is at hand.

Static disrupts the sacred harmonies.
Things are thrown at things with wedges of thunder.
Today's Special: bananas and ketchup,
but never the special things.

THE ONION AND THE PIANO

It's not Dada to put together a piano with an onion, it's
easy to do, like painting any kind of landscape, or
speaking with a tongue split in two. On the window ledge
as you pass, a bowl with an onion in it is
a pale white inside a pale blue, and an etude
coming out, between curtains dotted red on yellow,
mixes with the smell of dinner, dancing and desire.

You make it up. You are playing a fife while
an enemy joins you on his piano. Behind you
there's a painting on the wall, "Girl With Onions." You once
loved her and associated everything with her smell.
You are drawing with chalk a rubble of onions thrown against a
      wall,
using every color you have to get the right white while
standing on a piano. Two pianos. You are standing in a field

of tomatoes and one onion sprout intrudes, dominating the view.
You hear the tinkling, too close to reality,
of an eighteenth-century harpsichord (not a piano?)
playing boogie-woogie thought up by Bach
in the shadowy intensity of the world between your ears.
Your coloring book growingly has no meaning—
you interchange the colors every day.
There's a ballerina on a giant onion, rolling

between laughter and her fancy feet. She is telling us
that there's a symbolic mystery under her movements
and the luminous ball she dances on, which has been
painted as an obvious fake of cardboard, confetti and paste,

with hints of layers of skin and the color of breaking waves,
that an onion, if it moves and is cold, could be an ocean.

Or almost anything (except by fact or fantasy) a piano.
Even the keys are an off-match, the legs impossible
the sound coming out of it never an onion sound,
not an etude for a tangy vegetable, unless you can allow,
as in a poem or cartoon, onions to possess voices singing
within the range of strings, pedals and soft hammers.

Merging into sight in the sky are two separated things,
a musician with his neck broken playing on an flattened onion
as if it were a violin, and under him the grass cups a blue ox
into a bowl with no meaning. You accept it, nodding your head
to the music. You are starved for improbabilities. There are
never enough in your life, between the ads

for cars high up on mesas and cures for erectile dysfunction,
fungus, bad breath and indigestion, any two will do.
It is like marriages that are needed. Some last, some don't.
There is surrealism in the air we breathe. Two
impossibilities, like rocks and branches, fit together
in the same landscape. They can kill you or help you live.

Thunder sobs next to the radio when it hears its big voice
reduced on a recording of a storm whose raindrops
share only stories of rain. However you look,
the piano and the onion are just lightning and hail,
mixing it up for equilibrium, endless shades of what's for real.

RED DUST

Filmed on location, but with trouble
finding the right Chinaman, with naivete and dignity,
who could relate realistically with the blond
filing her nails in the wilderness.
Everyone was out of place
on the Indochinese rubber plantation.

Would you have liked to slap the Overseer's wife,
Mary Astor on the hunt, or tell the Big Lug
to say "Nuts!" to both women who fought for him,
to go into the jungle with his knife and kill the tiger
the only thing that really belonged on the set
so the movie could get on with its marvellous life?

D-DAY AT THE BEACH

You have not quite decided on anything.
It does not matter.
Decisions are everywhere, to the right,
to the left, you can wade
through them as you approach the shore.
Their little whitecaps break
against the back of your knees.

The scramble to reach the beach
delays the decision, if
delay is what you have allowed as important,
not now the choice between the freedom
to let yourself float
face down in your decision or to play
on the sands until you're old enough to care.

SIDE TWO OF SIDE ONE

There is a space between Heaven and Hell.
I found it at 503–4916 on my cellphone.
When you retune your radio
dial Station 563
just part way from 536 near somebody's
exciting, dark zero.

Don't let the ads gull you.
The telephone solicitation for love is a feint
and the radio's murmur that you can buy more via
arm spray and springless mattresses is a ploy.
Stay tuned out halfway through. Unplug the void.
Hang up exactly right there.

Our hands flap for beauty like bats
off at sunset.
Our hands live in caves
made to fumble along the dark
for a different beauty.
It flies away.

If you look in the mirror there is
a space between Heaven and Hell.
Focus on the background
where the closet door
is half-open from the night before,
where a nightgown hangs that is not yours.

Turn on the CD.
What's left of your dream
is on the other side of the label—
the lack of excitement, the busy signals,
the static and the hanging bats.
Music squeaks
up and down scales and even
the closet door opens both ways.

CHOKE POINT

The choke point can be reached
through romance movies
log jams, street crossings or
neckties
encircled by hands.

It can rise up from nowhere
overcome by grief
a death wish or
a bone stuck in your best joke.
Don't try

to remove it by yourself or call
the Red Cross.
They're busy at terrible
intersections
far-flung.

If it delays your trip
work it out
don't jump off
stay with it until
you make it to Greenland's vast mountains

vacant islands or (why not)
any uninhabited space
with or without animals
where you can bury your face
in enormous emptinesses of sorrow

once the road ends
and dumps you.
It's a round trip and your seat should be
free
of stuff
for the ride back.

THE RED SUNDIAL

In the middle of the sundial
the shadows move like hands
blackened in a birdbath
on a hot day of windows
whose tongues pant like blue curtains
against yellowed paint on four sides.

How often we build things
that are not meant as intended
a wedding caught in a bottle's round mirror
on a day of mourning
when the church rises up in smoke
to give a rosary of burnt offerings.

Like a need for necessity
or the hope for hopelessness
a relationship ends in smoke and mirrors with
sun spiked on the red spire
of a sundial, Gloria Patri,
on a hot 1:32 PM, Nebraska.

POEMS ALONG THE WALL

To those who practice this satisfaction of gathering honey,
a great flood of sugar or almost any sweet
substitute word
could wash us away into droplets of many ecstasies.
You know, to those
who remember the moment of a petal's jangle along a wall
against ankle or fellow flower
sweet to eye and ear
taste cannot follow such feelings in motion
or sounds in blossom.

My own writing exists in a lusty pool
I am constantly refilling
from older, vanishing pages,
stepping back into a warmer sweetness.
See the honey wash into my words? As if
bees had been practicing satisfaction
by keeping to themselves
the honey they made out of far landscapes,
as I should, too,
with a labour of my tongue savoring
ancestors and errors
thick and slow,
bitterness edging the sweetness,
new petals humming over rough, lonely fingers.

POET'S PEPPER TREE

Because I never wrote it,
your poem is better than mine.
Your birds have more color. Their songs
climb up the down branches
of tall, weeping trees
the way clever birds might
if that was their reason.

They eat peppers
pink in their beaks.
The wind ruffles their vanity.
Right next to the scribbled sheets
of green spaces
you wrote to melancholy,
my joy erupts
like a vowel sound
upside down

screeching our wedding song.
I chew on your life on
your red cheeks
on the tongue in your head
that keeps ideas
spit at me
like seeds.

My jealousy for birds that are not mine
burns my groin.
I envy them climbing
up and down with their peppers
pink in their beaks. I envy
a wind that can ruffle the vanity
of whole birds
flying from bitterness.

BORDER CROSSINGS

As early as possible, we cross the border.
It's illegal. We look both ways.
The reason, not clear, is to cross for security's sake, say
marriage, margaritas, money, or food.

I patted the horse in the dark.
I said, it's some kind of test, boy, for both of us.
Go slow, because all we're trying to do
is exchange the moons.

The eagles ditch their toenails in the zoos.
The rattlesnake circles itself like a mango seed.
Your hands grab at yourself for shelter.
Car radios pass car radios singing out
honeymoon accents.

I'm watching an illegal crossing nearby,
It's stealing one shoe of a pair.
I used to think I owned the Hedge in The Garden
that kept me there.

Even if you get a free pass
Your feet will go flat from punctures.
Look. Wind flirting with dust. Incompatible.
And the doves want more doves and more crackers.

The invention of governments led us to these endless parties
celebrating broken borders.
Marriages, entombments, graduations.
Over three thousand borders a day invade us!

At least I've still got the horse
who thinks he belongs to Roy Rodgers
because I sing so sweet at the sunsets
each time we watch that movie.

MY FAVORITE BLOND(E)

Take your credit cards when you go shopping.
Near the back of the mall
where few look
they're selling ready-made, off-the-rack strangers.
Buy as many as you like
for the sake of convenience.

Then, it's party time.
Take your new friends to the theater.
That old Madeleine Carroll movie—
a black and white miracle.
When it's over you'll see
those credits are still up there rolling
and your own credit balance has doubled.

After the bus takes you home
and you're in your pajamas
the memory of those kisses on your side
of the screen
will entertain you long after the projector
has shown the death of winter
and the spring sales start up again.

ANOTHER LOOK AT THE GARDEN

The window has glass in it
the garden has not.
There's a path between grass
but the grass is not a path.
Fairies are not paying attention
at what you see outside which is
not the inside for the inside
is invented
but the outside was.

If the world is not a dream
is a dream not the world?
Are you looking at a map to find where you are?
The fairies are sitting over there by Asia
inside and out, in every bedroom
and haystack. They are part of nature now
the way love has become fabric.

They were not asked to share our sofas,
but once an idea is needed
it spreads like salt and sugar. They are
riding in our automobiles,
eating our dinners. We say
"I don't see them!" as they go by like buses.
There's a fire
burning inside our fireplaces, the inside is,
is burning the outside.
And you stand getting warm like an angel
before a mirror full of furies.

WOOF

Can I sublet your headphones
or rent the vacancy of music empty of your voice
but held over?
I'll climb any tough soundtrack,
hold your hat to check your headgear.
Churches make amends for steeples.
Pealing.

Pride hangs us between off and on, all made up
as we go along.
I'll rhyme words like hot and cool
make a slow song hit 80 in reverse
yell it back to you full throttle
to race the dead.

They're still broadcasting your favorite.
It's thumping by the riverside.
It's about
that time you circled back while I slept.
What I pick up isn't rust,
dried songs or your discarded footprints

I pick up where you used to die,
the vibration
doesn't stop. A long time ago
before the bullrushes came
the music only pretended
it turned you off.

SENTENCING

First you have to end it
if you want to begin. rain before clouds and the exit
is where the subway enters.

The judge who sentences us is smiling.
He knows a crime is uncommitted.
After his judgement.
I left. So our tears will flow to no subject or object.

A verb runs around naked. If you sentence me
is that a letter?
Verbs sound like someway cars rumbling
I love you,
The "Don't Start" is the ending.

A judge swapped our I.D.s
That's when the irregular sentences bumped and
"Pardon me" was like soup for dessert. Kisses without crime
can't make moral judgements.

Soft commas of separation
turn to steel bars.

At the station the someway keeps muttering
I love you, I love you, I love you, I love you

the subject, the object arrive
get on to get off. Judges mostly.

That was beautiful it felt so good,
Verbs blushing before the big act,
before they take off their costumes to play roles.

Try speaking without a verb screaming at you.
Try stopping the way it begins.

ON THE ROAD

Landscapes invented come in Mays. Junes
are different, little footfalls talking together
through teen leaves wanting to grow up
and repeat everything. Most things
look different from our thoughts of them.
We put ourselves together
"folding and folding" as one Robin says.

How exciting, and the great cars
with mirrored faces sneak by like futures
of sharks past each month. No surprise speeches.
Rediscovery is all that's about. You can
count your Mays on your fingers
waving flattened out toward sand hills on the shore's stop. Last year
    wasn't bad.

The future was softer, but the wind
hit harder against its enemies, toppling
trees, houses, animals, entranceways
and all our friends—pushed us
against a wall. Chunks of words
melted down the street back to sea.
As they splash, even bareness loves your Mays,
awninged storefronts, too, won't have
your speedings be alone. Then
you went back into hiding always jealous
of trees blooming and things amazingly
prettier than you.

After wading, words float back. Little periods,
dots in dresses, take long spaces and pause

before diving into the wind's web
rare leaping to make this appearance
for shorelines that Mays open to
spreading into a fertilized falling
for Junes.

I hope you can read this while
you dust your house. Junes comes
too quickly after Mays, sweats dry as soon
as it hits the page. Call it the end
of a chapter when it can't be finished.
Things will look different in June.
Bare in mind the better May,
crushed as a cupcake all-time flowering.

A PRISM OF BIRDS

1.

The morning's portion of violets—
basing the future on a schedule of arriving flowers.
The day began with the mandatory thunderstorms
always in the distance
birds disturbing the rhododendrons below the window
my attention shifts to the vase
holding the flowers
holding no birds, no thunder, no feeling
except as I fill it.
If you came into the room
for any reason
I would put you in the vase
rejecting the violets
the Fall schedule
the fullness of my emptiness.

2.

Since they had nothing to say, they talked about
the weather, the birds and the cost of living—
how cold the money had become, as if the souls had flown
from it.
He looked her in the eyes and considered
what it might be like to hold her hand
but the thought flew off.
He said, "My farm might not make the expenses this year."

She saw the fright in his eyes
like a death wish for a wounded hawk.
Reaching out her hand she

swooped in
cold as money
cold as the weather cost him.

3.

When the snowbirds come they cover everything
they settle on the rooftops
they are trying to get warm
instead they warm the earth
like a quilt. A quilt muffles us.
The birds rise just as we are used to them
we can hear the train in the station
whoo whoo goes the sound
now broken out of the feathers
sound is everywhere the cold is
on your two faces of snow
a fairytale read by Hitler
and the voice marches with its troops
who whoo they are everywhere
displacing the cold again.

LANDIS EVERSON was born in 1926 in Coronado, California, and now lives in San Luis Obispo, California. He was a member of the Berkeley Renaissance of the late 1940s, alongside his friends Jack Spicer, Robin Blaser and Robert Duncan. While completing a Master's in English at Columbia in 1951, he encountered John Ashbery, who would later publish a selection of his poems in *Locus Solus*. In 1955, while Karl Shapiro's teaching assistant at Berkeley, Everson had the first of four appearances in *Poetry*. In 1960, he participated in a weekly poetry group with Spicer and Blaser in San Francisco, and wrote the sequences "Postcard from Eden" and "The Little Ghosts I Played With." He then stopped writing for 43 years. His rediscovery by poet and editor Ben Mazer, whose anthology of the Berkeley Renaissance in *Fulcrum* 3 (2004) printed Everson's poetry for the first time since 1962, and the friendship that ensued between the two poets, prompted Everson to begin writing again. Since then his many remarkable new poems have appeared in *Poetry*, *New Yorker*, *London Review of Books*, *Fulcrum*, *New Republic*, *American Poetry Review*, *Chicago Review*, *Jacket* and elsewhere. In October 2005, the Poetry Foundation (Chicago) honored Everson with the first Emily Dickinson Award, for a poet over fifty who has never published a book of poems. This is his winning collection and long overdue first book, *Everything Preserved: Poems 1955–2005*.

Everything Preserved has been typeset in Adobe Garamond, a font drawn by Robert Slimbach and based on type cut by Claude Garamond in the sixteenth century. Book design by Wendy Holdman. Composition by Prism Publishing Center, and manufactured by Versa Press on acid-free paper.